ShowTime® Piano

Jazz & Blues

2011 Edition

Level 2A

Elementary Playing

This book belongs to: _____

Arranged by

Nancy and Randall Faber

Production Coordinator: Jon Ophoff
Cover: Terpstra Design, San Francisco
Engraving: Dovetree Productions, Inc.

FABER
PIANO ADVENTURES®
3042 Creek Drive
Ann Arbor, Michigan 48108

T0020219

A NOTE TO TEACHERS

ShowTime® Piano Jazz & Blues is a spirited collection of jazz and blues pieces. The book offers a pleasing variety of sounds—from soulful blues to jazz originals and standards—and is a wonderful supplement for the Level 2A piano student. The student will enjoy creating the sounds of jazz and blues while improving reading and rhythmic skills.

ShowTime® Jazz & Blues is part of the *ShowTime® Piano* series. "ShowTime" designates Level 2A of the *PreTime®* to *BigTime®* piano library arranged by Faber and Faber.

Following are the levels of the supplementary library, which lead from *PreTime®* to *BigTime®*.

PreTime® Piano	(Primer Level)
PlayTime® Piano	(Level 1)
ShowTime® Piano	(Level 2A)
ChordTime® Piano	(Level 2B)
FunTime® Piano	(Level 3A – 3B)
BigTime® Piano	(Level 4)

Each level offers books in a variety of styles, making it possible for the teacher to offer stimulating material for every student. For a complimentary detailed listing, e-mail faber@pianoadventures.com or write us at the mailing address below.

Visit **www.PianoAdventures.com**.

Helpful Hints:

1. At the *ShowTime®* level the student begins to move out of a 5-finger position. A circled finger number is used to alert the student to a change of hand position.

2. Many jazz and blues pieces use *swing rhythm*. Here, the quarter note beat is divided into a long and then a short eighth note, rather than being equally divided. It is approximately the same as $\text{♩}^3\text{♪}$. Use this "lilting" of the eighth notes whenever the tempo marking says *swing*.

3. Optional teacher duets are a valuable part of the *ShowTime® Piano* series, and these provide rhythmic vitality and harmonic interest.

About Jazz & Blues

Jazz and blues are distinctively American styles of music, characterized by improvisation and syncopated rhythm. Blues—an ancestor of jazz—can be traced back to the days of slavery, when American blacks began to combine African melodies and rhythms with Western harmony.

At the turn of the century, ragtime's syncopated rhythm took the country by storm—in fact Scott Joplin's piano rags were best sellers in his day. As blues and ragtime styles influenced each other, a dynamic swing style emerged which eventually became known as jazz. Championed in New Orleans by Jelly Roll Morton and Louis Armstrong, the new sound soared in popularity. By the 1920s, jazz had entered the mainstream of American popular music.

During the Swing Era of the 1930s and 40s, people were dancing to the big band sounds of Glenn Miller and other band leaders. The cool sounds of bebop followed in the 1950s, a time when solo artists such as Miles Davis and Charlie Parker infused jazz with a new seriousness—and ever since then jazz has continued to grow and change. Today the influence of blues and jazz can be heard in almost all popular music.

ISBN 978-1-61677-045-7

TABLE OF CONTENTS

You Are the Sunshine of My Life

Words and Music by
STEVIE WONDER

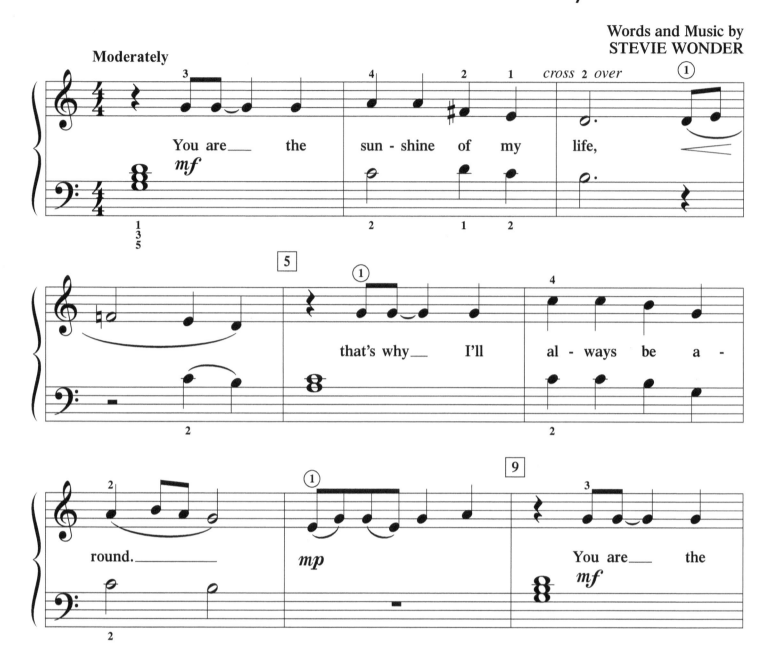

Teacher Duet: (Student plays 1 octave higher)

Bye Bye Blackbird

Lyric by MORT DIXON

Music by RAY HENDERSON

Teacher Duet: (Student plays 1 octave higher)

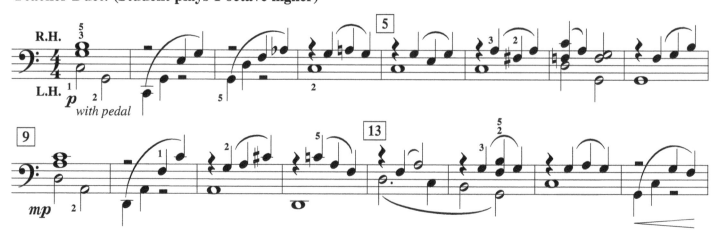

Swingin' Sam

Music by
NANCY FABER

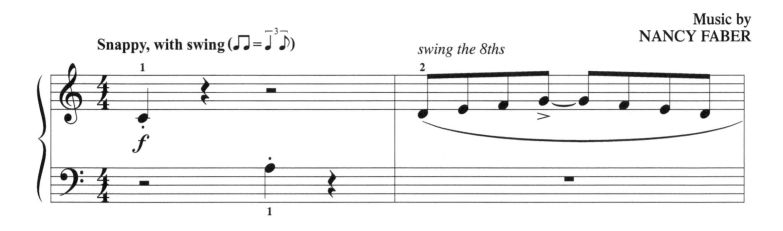

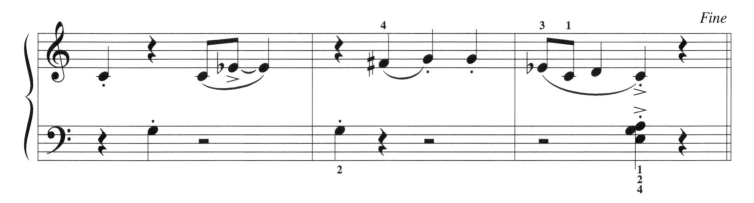

Teacher Duet: (Student plays 1 octave higher)

Blue Moon

Words by LORENZ HART

Music by RICHARD RODGERS

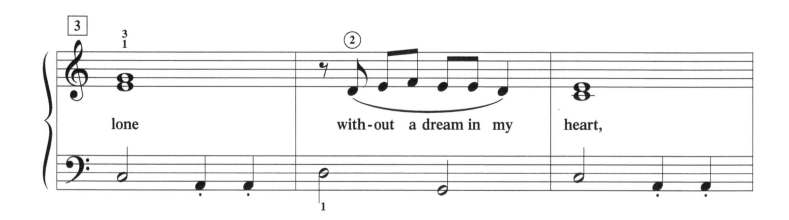

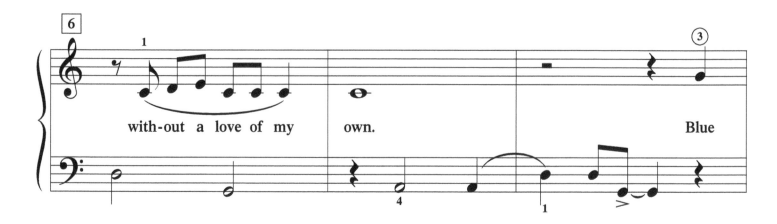

Teacher Duet: (Student plays as written)

From *THE MUPPET MOVIE*

The Rainbow Connection

Words and Music by PAUL WILLIAMS
and KENNETH L. ASCHER

Moderately, with a lilt

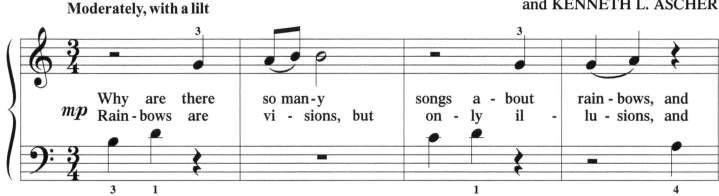

Why are there   so man-y   songs a-bout   rain-bows, and
Rain-bows are   vi - sions, but   on - ly il -   lu-sions, and

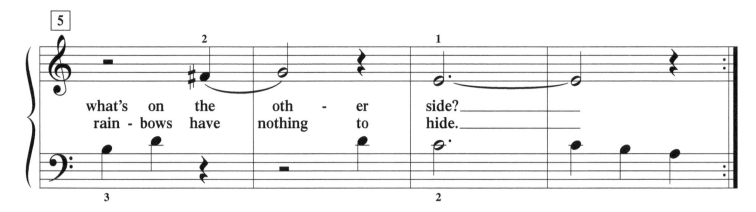

what's   on   the   oth - er   side?
rain - bows   have   nothing   to   hide.

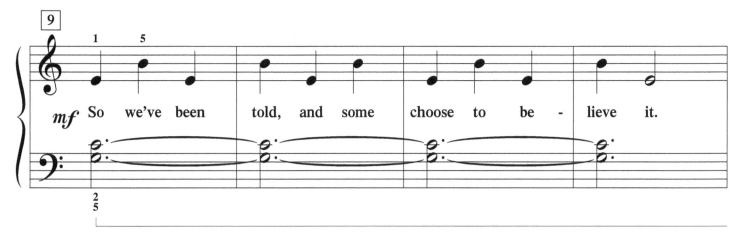

mf So   we've   been   told, and   some   choose   to   be -   lieve   it.

Teacher Duet: (Student plays 1 octave higher)

R.H.

L.H.

p with pedal

Mama Don't 'Low

TRADITIONAL BLUES

Mama don't 'low no guitar pick-in' 'round here.

Mama don't 'low no guitar pick-in' 'round here.

Teacher Duet: (Student plays 1 octave higher)

Oh, You Beautiful Doll

Words by A. SEYMOUR BROWN
Music by NAT D. AYER

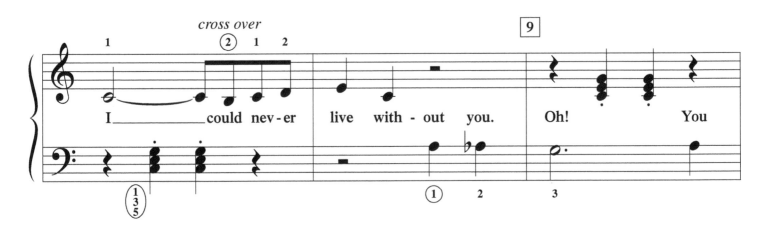

Teacher Duet: (Student plays 1 octave higher)

From *OKLAHOMA!*

The Surrey with the Fringe on Top

Lyrics by OSCAR HAMMERSTEIN II
Music by RICHARD RODGERS

Teacher Duet: (Student plays 1 octave higher)

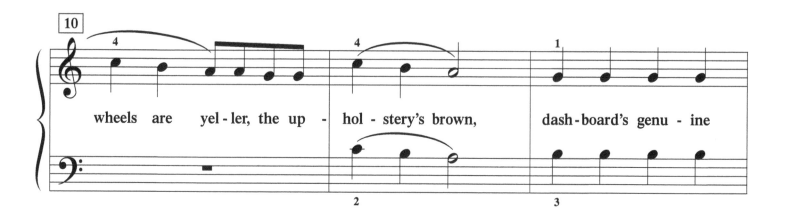

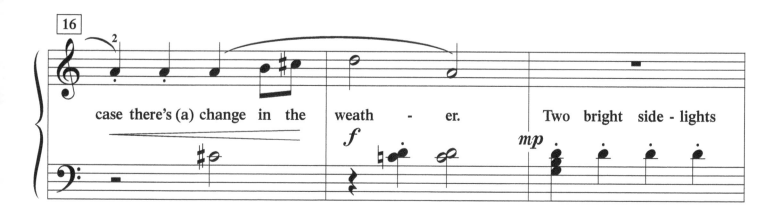

When the Red, Red Robin Comes Bob, Bob Bobbin' Along

Words and Music by
HARRY WOODS

Teacher Duet: (Student plays 1 octave higher)

Loco-music-motion

Words and Music by
NANCY FABER